Preface ✍ W9-AAY-892

In the last 16 years, I have helped over 10,000 project managers in my workshops obtain their PMP® credential.

As some of you are aware, I am a second-degree black belt in Taekwondo.

Some people in martial arts practice kicking boards enough to ensure they can eventually break a board. I practice kicking boards over and over to ensure I will always break the board, every single time.

What if we could apply the same idea to preparing for the PMP® Exam? What if instead of practicing sample questions enough to get some of them right.... we practiced sample questions enough to never get any of them wrong?

For me the best way to prepare for the PMP® exam is through hundreds, if not thousands of sample questions.

I hope this mini e-book helps you really focus your studies to ensure you never get any contract calculation questions wrong again.

If you like what you read in this book please leave an honest review on Amazon so that others can join our successful PMP community.

About the Author

Aileen Ellis, PgMP®, PMP®, is The PMP® Expert. She is the owner and proudly the only instructor for AME Group Inc., a Registered Education Provider (REP®) through the Project Management Institute (PMI®). She personally instructs project managers to gain the confidence and knowledge to pass the PMP® Exam, the CAPM® Exam and the PgMP® Exam. She has helped more than 10,000 professionals obtain their PMP® and over 1,000 professionals obtain those coveted letters: CAPM®. Working with thousands of students from dozens of countries, Ms. Ellis has gained a thorough understanding of the ins and outs of the PMBOK® Guide, the exam content, and proven test-taking strategies.

Ms. Ellis began teaching Exam Preparation Courses in 1998. Over the years she has mastered how students learn best and has incorporated those lessons and methods into her books. Her approach is focused on understanding the Project Management Processes and their interactions, with limited memorization. Ms. Ellis not only leads workshops to help students study for and pass the CAPM®, PMP®, and PgMP® exams through review of content and hundreds of sample questions, she provides materials (books, sample questions) to other REP®s and PMI® Chapters to support their educational efforts.

Set Up of the book

Part One - Some basic ideas on Contract Types and a few short videos. Don't skip the videos. They will really help with understanding the ideas.

Part Two - 50+ Contract Calculation Questions. My suggestion is that you take notes on paper as you are working through these questions. Absolutely write down the answer you chose and why you chose that answer.

Part Three - 50+ Detailed Solutions. Make sure you review every question so that when you see questions similar to these questions on the PMP® Exam you are sure you will get every single one right. Good Luck.

Part One

The three categories of contracts are:
1. **Fixed Price**
2. **Cost Reimbursable** – This category is sometimes called Cost Plus.
3. **Time and Materials** – This category is a hybrid of the Fixed price and the Cost reimbursable categories.

We will look at each category as a whole and the contract types inside each category. The list of contract types provided here is not all-inclusive. There may be other contract types in a category but they are not listed here since it is unlikely they will be on the PMP® Exam.

Fixed Price category - Here are a few key points concerning the Fixed price category.

- The seller is obligated to deliver to the requirements. If the seller cannot meet the requirements the seller may incur financial damages.
- The Statement of work (SOW) should be clear and measureable. The SOW should not be open ended.
- The buyer has less financial risk than the seller. The buyer does not need to make payment to the seller unless the seller is able to meet the requirements.
- The seller has more financial risk than the buyer. The seller could lose money on a fixed price contract if he is unable to meet the requirements or if the cost to do the work is higher than he projected.

Let's look at three types inside the Fixed Price category.

Firm Fixed Price (FFP)

The buyer and the seller agree to a fixed price for the contract. If the seller completes the work for less than the fixed price the seller makes a profit. If the seller completes the work for more than the fixed price of the contract the seller takes a loss.

FFP is the lowest risk contract type for a buyer. FFP is the highest risk contract type for a seller. Some will say that the share ratio on a FFP contract is 0/100%. The buyer has 0% of the contract risk and the seller has 100% of the contract risk.

Fixed Price Incentive Fee (FPIF)
Here is a short video on the elements of a FPIF
and how to solve an FPIF calculation problem.
If you have a hard copy version of this book go
to www.aileenellis.com/blog for all my videos.

This contract type is sometimes called Fixed
Price Incentive (FPI). In this book I will use both
terms so there are no surprises for you on the
PMP® Exam.
While this contract is in the fixed price category,
the final price of the contract is not fixed unless
the seller's costs reach the price ceiling.

The buyer and seller agree to multiple elements
if a FPIF contract:

Target cost - this is what the buyer and seller
believe it will cost the seller to complete the
contract
Target profit - this is what the buyer and seller
agree is a reasonable profit based on the target
cost and the type/amount of risk taken by the
seller
Target price = target cost + target profit

Ceiling price - this is the upper limit on what the
buyer will pay for the product/service. If the
seller's costs go higher than the ceiling price the
buyer will only be required to pay the ceiling
price. The ceiling price protects the buyer.

Share ratio - listed as two numbers that add to
100%.
Let's take an example of a share ration of
70/30%. The buyer's share is always listed first.
The seller's share is always listed last.

Share ratio in an under run situation - If the seller were to under run the target cost (finish the work for less than the target cost) then 30% of the under run would go to the seller as additional profit.

Share ratio in an overrun situation - If the seller were to overrun the target cost then 30% of the overrun would be paid by the seller (through a decreased profit).

PTA - Point of total assumption for a FPIF contract

Here is a short video on how to solve for PTA. If you have a hard copy version of this book go to www.aileenellis.com/blog for all my videos.

The PTA is the point in which the seller assumes all the cost risk. The PTA is not something the buyer and the seller negotiate. The PTA is calculated based on the other elements of the contract.   When the actual costs are below the PTA the buyer and seller share the risk according to the share ratio. Once the actual costs hit the PTA the share ratio turns to 0/100 % with the buyer owning zero percent of the risk and the seller owning 100% of the risk.
For the PMP® Exam know the following equation:

PTA = Target Cost + ((Ceiling Price-Target Price)/ Buyer's Share)

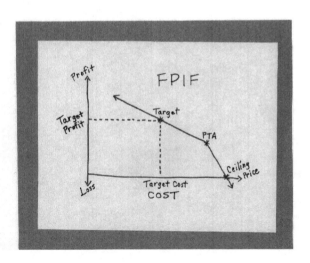

Fixed Price with economic price adjustment (FP-EPA)

The buyer and seller agree to certain terms and conditions often related to items outside of the control of the seller. Examples of these items may include the cost of commodities, the cost of certain types of labor, inflation costs, etc. An outside financial indicator will determine the final price of these items.

While this contract is in the fixed price category the final price of the contract is not fixed. We see this contract type more often on longer contracts and in situations where the market lacks stability.

Cost reimbursable category - Here are a few key points concerning the cost reimbursable category.

- The seller is obligated to put forth their best effort.
- The Statement of work (SOW) should allow for flexibility to redirect the seller.
- The buyer has more financial risk than the seller. The buyer must reimburse for all legitimate actual costs plus a fee. Fee here means seller's profit.
- The seller has less financial risk than the buyer. The seller has all their legitimate actual costs reimbursed plus receives a fee (profit).

Cost Plus Incentive Fee (CPIF)

Here is a short video on the elements of a CPIF and how to solve a CPIF math problem. If you have a hard copy version of this book go to www.aileenellis.com/blog for all my videos.

The cost plus incentive fee contract is sometimes called Cost Plus Incentive (CPI).

The buyer and seller agree to multiple elements:
Target cost - This is what the buyer and seller believe it will cost the seller to complete the contract.
Target fee - This is what the buyer and seller agree is a reasonable fee based on the target cost and the type/amount of risk taken by the seller.
Note the term target price is often **not** used in the industry in relation to a CPIF contract.

There is no ceiling price on a CPIF contract. Since there is no ceiling price there is no Point of total assumption (PTA) on a CPIF contract. (Be careful of this as many PMP® Prep books have wrong information in this area).

Minimum fee - The minimum fee the seller will receive if the seller completes the work.
Maximum fee - The maximum fee the seller will receive if the seller completes the work. In some organizations the maximum fee is limited to no more than 15% of the target cost.

Share ratio - Sharing occurs between the minimum and maximum fee. The ratio is listed as two numbers that add up to 100%.

Let's take an example of a share ration of 70/30%. The buyer's share is always listed first. The seller's share is always listed last.

Share ratio in an under run situation - If the seller were to under run the target cost (finish the work for less than the target cost) then 30% of the under run would go to the seller as an additional fee.   This would be true unless the calculated fee is greater than the maximum fee. If the calculated fee is greater than the maximum fee the seller will receive the maximum fee.

Share ratio in an overrun situation - If the seller were to overrun the target cost then 30% of the overrun would be paid by the seller (through a decreased profit). This would be true unless this fee is less than the minimum fee. If this calculated fee is less than the minimum fee the seller will receive the minimum fee.

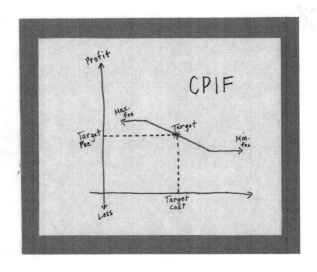

Cost Plus Award Fee (CPAF)

The buyer and seller agree to multiple elements in a CPAF Contract:

Estimated cost - What the buyer and the seller estimate it will cost the seller to complete the work.

Base fee - The minimum profit the seller will receive. It is often between 0% and 3% of the estimated (not actual) costs.

Award fee - The amount of the profit that is based on some broad subjective criteria. Often up to 12 % of the estimated (not actual) costs.

Max Fee = base fee + the award fee. The Max Fee is usually not more than 15% of the estimated (not actual) costs.

Fee determination period - The time period that the fee will be calculated and payment made. Examples include one time per month or one time every three months.

There needs to be an **award fee plan** that explains the why and the how of the award fee program.

A few key ideas related to CPAF Contracts

The criteria for the award fee is subjective not objective.

The customer decides unilaterally how much of an award fee that the seller will receive based on the rules in the award fee plan.

The primary reason a buyer would use a CPAF contract is to ensure that the seller's objectives are always in line with the buyer's objectives.

Cost Plus Fixed Fee (CPFF)
Here is a short video on the elements of a CPFF contract and the elements of a Cost plus percentage cost (CPPC) contract.
If you have a hard copy version of this book go to www.aileenellis.com/blog for all my videos.

These two contract types are often confused with each other.

The buyer and the seller agree to multiple elements in a CPFF contract:

Estimated cost - What the buyer and the seller estimate it will cost the seller to complete the work.
Fixed fee - The buyer and seller will then look at the nature of the work as well as other parameters to determine a reasonable fee. Fee means profit. This fee is a percentage of the estimated costs. This fee now changes from a percentage of the estimated costs to a fixed number. The fixed fee is the profit paid to the supplier. It does not change, regardless of the seller's actual legitimate costs unless there is a change in scope.

Let's take an example of a fixed fee in a CPFF.
The buyer and seller agree that the estimated cost for a project is $100. Based on the nature of the work they agree that the seller should receive a 10% fee (meaning profit) for the work. 10% of $100 = $10. The $10 now becomes the fixed fee. It is no longer a percentage. The seller completes the work for an actual cost of $80. The seller receives $10 in fee. The seller does not receive 10% of the actual cost of $80 in fee.

Cost plus percentage cost (CPPC)

This contract type is not discussed in the PMBOK® Guide. It is possible, though not likely, that it will be on the PMP® Exam.

The buyer and seller agree to multiple elements in a CPPC contract:

Estimated cost - What the buyer and the seller estimate it will cost the seller to complete the work.

Fee percentage - This percentage is equal to a percentage of the actual (not the target) costs that will be awarded in the fee.

Some organizations do not allow the use of a CPPC contract type as it provides a **negative incentive** to the contract costs. The more the seller spends the greater their fee (their profit).

CPFF vs. CPPC

Cost Plus Fixed Free
  Estimated cost = $100
  Fixed Fee = $10

CPFF			
Actual Cost	$80	$100	$120
Fee	$10	$10	$10
Actual Price	$90	$110	$130

Cost Plus % Cost
  Estimated cost = $100
  Fee % = 10 %

CPPC			
Actual Cost	$80	$100	$120
Fee	$8	$10	$12
Actual Price	$88	$110	$132

Time and Materials (T&M) Contracts - These contracts are really a hybrid of a fixed price and a cost reimbursable contract.

Fixed price element: The buyer will pay a fixed price per hour or day for labor.
Cost reimbursable elements:
The buyer will reimburse material costs at cost. The buyer does not know the exact number of hours the work will take and therefore the final price of the contract is not fixed.

Ideas for Questions on Risk

These contract types are listed in order from lowest risk for the buyer (highest risk for the seller) to highest risk for the buyer (lowest risk for the seller).

Firm Fixed Price (FFP) – lowest risk for buyer and highest risk for seller.

Fixed Price Incentive Fee (FPIF)

Fixed Price Economic Price Adjustment (FP-EPA)

Cost Plus Award Fee (CPAF)

Cost Plus Incentive Fee (CPIF)

Cost Plus Fixed Fee (CPFF)

Cost Plus Percentage Cost (CPPC) –highest risk for the buyer and lowest risk for the seller.

Note that Time and Materials contracts are not on this list. Most people will agree that a buyer has higher risk and a seller has the lower risk on a T&M contract. There may be much disagreement though on where exactly to put the T&M on the list above.

Test Tip- make sure you know if you are the buyer or the seller in questions that ask about contract risk.

Rent versus Buy Questions

You will find several sample math questions that ask to determine when it makes sense to rent a piece of equipment versus when it makes sense to buy a piece of equipment.

To solve these problems, you want to set up an equation in which the cost to rent multiplied by the number of days = the investment to buy + the cost to operate multiplied by the number of days.

(Cost to rent) * days = investment cost +((cost to operate) * (number of days)).

I really do not think of this as an equation to memorize for the PMP® Exam. I think of it more as an idea to understand.
Realize that the equation above assumes the cost to rent is the full cost to rent. Read the questions carefully.

Part Two

1. You are trying to decide if you should rent or buy a piece of equipment for your project. The cost to rent per day is $300. The cost to purchase the piece of equipment is $14,000 plus $50 per day to operate. After how many days does the cost to rent equal the cost to buy?

a. 56 days
b. 62 days
c. 73 days
d. 84 days

2. A Fixed Price Incentive Fee (FPIF) Contract has the following parameters:

Target Cost = $100,000
Target Profit = $10,000
Target Price = $110,000
Ceiling Price = $130,000
Share Ratio 80/20

The project was completed for an actual cost of $123,000. What is the point of total assumption (PTA)?

a. $110,000
b. $123,000
c. $125,000
d. $130,000

3. A Cost Plus Incentive Fee (CPIF) Contract has the following parameters:

Target Cost = $300,000
Target Fee = $30,000
Share Ratio 75/25%
Maximum Fee = $45,000
Minimum Fee = $15,000

The seller completes the work with the buyer's permission for an actual cost of $320,000. No additional scope was added to the project. What is the fee the seller receives?

a. $15,000
b. $20,000
c. $25,000
d. $30,000

4. As a buyer you would like to enter into a contract with a supplier that will entail
a tremendous amount of technical risk for the seller. You would prefer a firm fixed price contract but there is no seller willing to enter into that contract type because of the risky nature of the work. Also, the sellers who are bidding on the work are all relatively new startups without adequate accounting systems for accurate cost accounting. Most likely you will need to enter into what contract type?

a. Fixed price incentive (FPI)
b. Cost plus incentive fee (CPIF)
c. Cost plus fixed fee (CPFF)
d. Time and materials (T&M)

5. A Fixed Price Incentive Fee (FPIF) contract has the following parameters:
Target Cost = $200,000
Target Profit = $20,000
Target Price = $220,000
Ceiling Price = $250,000
Share Ratio 70/30

The project was completed for an actual cost of $170,000. What is the actual profit the seller receives?

a. $9,000
b. $11,000
c. $20,000
d. $29,000

6. Your organization is trying to decide if you should make a purchase using a Firm fixed price (FFP) arrangement or a Cost plus fixed fee (CPFF) arrangement. Which of the following factors would make you decide to use CPFF?

a. You want the lowest risk possible for your organization.

b. You want to not have to audit the seller's accounting system.

c. You want the seller to be legally obligated under the contract to deliver with financial damages available for non-delivery.

d. You want the ability to redirect the seller because the statement of work cannot be defined in detail at the beginning of the project.

7. A Cost Plus Incentive Fee (CPIF) contract has the following parameters:
Target Cost = $500,000
Target Fee = $45,000
Share Ratio   50/50%
Maximum Fee = $60,000
Minimum Fee = $30,000

The seller completes the work with the buyer's permission for an actual cost of $450,000. No additional scope was added to the project. What is the final price paid that the seller receives?

a. $470,000
b. $480,000
c. $510,000
d. $520,000

8. Your satellite launch project has been going well. Your customer seems pleased with all areas except cost. The actual cost is already higher than the target cost and the project is not complete. The contract manager tells you that you are nearing the point of total assumption. This concerns both you and your management. The point of total assumption (PTA) is the point when:

a. Your organization takes over the entire project cost risk.
b. Your customer takes over the entire project cost risk.
c. The share ratio goes to 100/0.
d. The cost risk is equally shared between your organization and the customer organization.

9. A Fixed Price Incentive Fee (FPIF) Contract has the following parameters:
Target Cost = $100,000
Target Profit = $10,000
Target Price = $110,000
Ceiling Price = $130,000
Share Ratio 80/20

The seller completes the work for an actual cost of $127,000. What is the total price paid to the seller?

a. $121,600
b. $127,000
c. $130,000
d. $131,600

10. We are entering into a long-term contract with a supplier. There are multiple commodity type items that will be delivered as part of this contract. We want a contract type where we can precisely adjust the final price based on an outside financial index. What contract type are we most likely to use?

a. Firm fixed price (FFP)
b. Fixed price incentive fee (FPIF)
c. Fixed price with economic price adjustment (FP-EPA)
d. Cost plus incentive fee (CPIF)

11. A Fixed Price Incentive Fee (FPIF) Contract has the following parameters:
Target Cost = $200,000
Target Profit = $20,000
Target Price = $220,000
Ceiling Price = $250,000
Share Ratio 70/30

The project was completed for an actual cost of $218,576. What is the point of total assumption (PTA)?

a. $238,576
b. $222,857
c. $262,857
d. $242,857

12. As a buyer you are trying to enter into a contract relationship with a low cost risk. The most likely contract type you will use is:

a. Time and materials (T&M)
b. Cost plus fixed fee (CPFF)
c. Cost plus incentive fee (CPIF)
d. Firm fixed price (FFP)

13. A Cost Plus Incentive Fee (CPIF) Contract has the following parameters:
Target Cost = $600,000
Target Fee = $60,000
Share Ratio 80/20%
Maximum Fee = $80,000
Minimum Fee = $40,000

The seller completes the work for an actual cost of $630,000. What is the total price the seller receives?

a. $720,000
b. $600,000
c. $696,000
d. $684,000

14. You are trying to decide if you should lease or purchase a piece of equipment for your project. The daily lease cost is $50. To purchase the equipment will require an investment of $3,000 plus $20 per day to operate. After how many days does the cost to lease equal the cost to purchase?

a. 30 days
b. 50 days
c. 70 days
d. 100 days

15. A Fixed Price Incentive Fee (FPIF) Contract has the following parameters:
Target Cost = $200,000
Target Profit = $20,000
Target Price = $220,000
Ceiling Price = $250,000
Share Ratio 70/30

The project was completed for an actual cost of $150,000. What is the actual profit the seller receives?

a. $35,000
b. $20,000
c. $15,000
d. $10,000

16. Your organization is entering into a Cost plus fixed fee (CPFF) contract with a new supplier. You are trying to explain how the fixed fee is developed. The best way to describe this is:

a. The fixed fee is a percentage of the actual costs.
b. The fixed fee is a percentage of the actual costs plus the actual profits.
c. The fixed fee is a percentage of the estimated costs.
d. The fixed fee is a percentage of the estimated costs plus the estimated profits.

17. A Cost Plus Incentive Fee (CPIF) Contract has the following parameters:
Target Cost = $96,000
Target Fee = $6,000
Share Ratio 90/10%
Maximum Fee = $8,000
Minimum Fee = $4,000

The seller completes the work for an actual cost of $86,000. What is the fee the seller receives?

a. $4,000
b. $5,000
c. $7,000
d. $8,000

18. You have signed a cost plus fixed fee (CPFF) with a supplier to perform some work for you. The contract parameters include:

Estimated cost: $100,000
Fixed Fee: $10,000.

The seller is able to complete the work for a cost of $120,000. The supplier had your permission to spend this amount of money. There is no change in scope. What is the final price paid to the supplier?

a. $100,000
b. $130,000
c. $132,000
d. $133,000

19. A Fixed Price Incentive Fee (FPIF) contract has the following parameters:
Target Cost = $100,000
Target Profit = $10,000
Target Price = $110,000
Ceiling Price = $130,000
Share Ratio 80/20

The seller completes the work for an actual cost of $128,000. What is the actual profit paid to the seller?

a. $0
b. $2,000
c. $4,400
d. $5,600

20. You are about to award a contract to a seller who will provide long-term product development and testing for a period of four years. Your organization is trying to decide between a Fixed Price Incentive Fee (FPIF) and a Cost Plus Incentive Fee (CPIF) contract. Which of the following is the major difference that separates a FPIF from a CPIF?

a. When the seller overruns the seller's profit is decreased.
b. When the seller under runs the seller's profit is increased.
c. There is a price ceiling to protect the buyer.
d. There is a share ratio that represents how the buyer and seller will share cost overruns and under runs.

21. A Fixed Price Incentive Fee (FPIF) Contract has the following parameters:

Target Cost = $1,000,000
Target Profit = $87,500
Target Price = $1,087,500
Ceiling Price = $1,150,000
Share Ratio 70/30

What is the point of total assumption (PTA)?

a. $1,089,286
b. $1,087,500
c. $1,031,242
d. $985,326

22. Your organization is making a large purchase. Your goal is to build a strong long-term relationship with the seller. It is imperative for the success of the project for the two organizations to work well together. You would like to provide incentives to the seller and at times these incentives will need to be quite subjective. You decide to set up a contract type that will ensure the seller's objectives are completely aligned with your objectives. The most likely contract type to do this is:

a. Cost plus award fee (CPAF)
b. Time and materials (T&M)
c. Fixed price incentive (FPI)
d. Cost plus incentive fee (CPIF)

23. A Cost Plus Incentive Fee (CPIF) Contract has the following parameters:
Target Cost = $100,000
Target Fee = $10,000
Share Ratio 70/30%
Maximum Fee = $12,000
Minimum Fee = $8,000

The seller completes the work with the buyer's permission for an actual cost of $120,000. No additional scope was added to the project. What is the fee the seller receives?

a. $4,000
b. $8,000
c. $10,000
d. $16,000

24. You are the project manager for an organization selling products and services to many different customers. In some contract types it is more important than others to have a clear definition of scope. Which contract type are you least likely to enter if you have concerns about an unclear scope definition?

a. Time and materials
b. Cost plus fixed fee
c. Cost plus incentive cost
d. Firm fixed price

25. A Fixed Price Incentive Fee (FPIF) Contract has the following parameters:
Target Cost = $100,000
Target Profit = $10,000
Target Price = $110,000
Ceiling Price = $130,000
Share Ratio 80/20

The seller completes the work for an actual cost of $90,000. What is the profit paid to the seller?

a. $2,000
b. $10,000
c. $12,000
d. $14,000

26. You are trying to decide if you should rent or buy a piece of equipment for your project. The daily cost to rent is $115. To buy the equipment will require an investment of $4,000 plus $35 per day to operate. After how many days does the cost to rent equal the cost to buy?

a. 30 days
b. 40 days
c. 50 days
d. 60 days

27. A Cost Plus Incentive Fee (CPIF) Contract has the following parameters:
Target Cost = $300,000
Target Fee = $30,000
Share Ratio 75/25%
Maximum Fee = $45,000
Minimum Fee = $15,000

The seller completes the work for an actual cost of $280,000. What is the final price the seller receives?

a. $295,000
b. $315,000
c. $325,000
d. $335,000

28. We are about to enter into a contract with a long-term supplier. Over the last several years the relationship with the supplier has been very positive. Because of this history we are entering into a contract that will span ten years. This represents the longest commitment our organization has ever made to a supplier. As we move forward with the contract we see tremendous market instability. There seems to be uncertainty for not just material costs but also for labor costs. Most likely we will enter into what type of contract?

a. Firm fixed price (FFP)
b. Cost plus percentage cost (CPPC)
c. Time and materials (T&M)
d. Fixed price with economic price adjustment (FP-EPA)

29. A Fixed Price Incentive Fee (FPIF) contract has the following parameters:
Target Cost = $200,000
Target Profit = $20,000
Target Price = $220,000
Ceiling Price = $250,000
Share Ratio 70/30

The seller completes the work for an actual cost of $240,000. What is the actual price paid to the seller?

a. $248,000
b. $250,000
c. $252,000
d. $272,000

30. Of the following contract types which one in general has the highest risk for the seller?

a. Firm fixed price (FFP)
b. Time and materials (T&M)
c. Cost plus fixed fee (CPFF)
d. Cost plus incentive fee (CPIF)

31. A Fixed Price Incentive Contract has the following parameters:
Target Cost = $400,000
Target Profit = $40,000
Target Price = $440,000
Ceiling Price = $500,000
Share Ratio 80/20

The project was completed for an actual cost of $442,183. What is the point of total assumption (PTA)?

a. $475,000
b. $442,183
c. $425,000
d. $415,000

32.   You are the project manager overseeing the transfer of technology into a new factory. The project is going well yet you underestimated the need for the specific labor of electricians and plumbers. You will need to augment your staff for several weeks to fill the gaps. At this point it is unclear exactly what work this specific labor will perform and exactly how much time you will need from them. Most likely you will use what contract type?

a. Firm fixed price
b. Fixed price incentive
c. Cost plus fixed fee
d. Time and materials

33. A Cost Plus Incentive Fee (CPIF) Contract has the following parameters:
Target Cost = $96,000
Target Fee = $6,000
Share Ratio 90/10
Maximum Fee = $8,000
Minimum Fee = $4,000

The seller completes the work with the buyer's permission for an actual cost of $106,000. No additional scope was added to the project. What is the final price the seller receives?

a. $100,000
b. $104,000
c. $111,000
d. $113,000

34. Your organization is about to award a contract and is trying to decide between a Cost plus award fee (CPAF) contract and a Cost plus incentive fee (CPIF) contract. Which of the following is true for the CPAF but not true for the CPIF?

a. The fee is based on broad subjective performance criteria.
b. The seller is reimbursed for all legitimate costs.
c. The buyer has flexibility to redirect the seller if the original statement of work was not clearly defined.
d. The seller is required to put forth their best effort to get reimbursed.

35. A Fixed Price Incentive Fee (FPIF) contract has the following parameters:
Target Cost = $100,000
Target Profit = $10,000
Target Price = $110,000
Ceiling Price = $130,000
Share Ratio 80/20

The seller completes the work for an actual cost of $80,000. What is the total price paid to the seller?

a. $80,000
b. $90,000
c. $94,000
d. $96,000

36. You are the project manager for a large government agency. Your organization requires a supplier to perform long-term research and development. You truly want the contractor to focus on the nature of the work and not be concerned with incentives. Most likely you will want what contract type?

a. Firm fixed price (FFP)
b. Cost plus award fee (CPAF)
c. Cost plus fixed fee (CPFF)
d. Time and materials (T&M)

37. A Cost Plus Incentive Fee (CPIF) Contract has the following parameters:
Target Cost = $600,000
Target Fee = $60,000
Share Ratio 80/20%
Maximum Fee = $65,000
Minimum Fee = $55,000

The seller completes the work for an actual cost of $570,000. What is the actual fee the seller receives?

a. $54,000
b. $55,000
c. $65,000
d. $66,000

38. Of the following contract types which one in general has the lowest risk for the seller?

a. Firm fixed price (FFP)
b. Cost plus percentage cost (CPPC)
c. Cost plus fixed fee (CPFF)
d. Cost plus incentive fee (CPIF)

39. A Fixed Price Incentive Fee (FPIF) contract has the following parameters:
Target Cost = $200,000
Target Profit = $20,000
Target Price = $220,000
Ceiling Price = $250,000
Share Ratio 70/30

The seller completes the work for an actual cost of $245,000. What is the actual profit paid to the seller?

a. $5,000
b. $6,500
c. $13,500
d. $33,500

40. You are trying to decide if you should rent or buy a piece of equipment for your project. The daily cost to rent is $80. To buy the equipment will require an investment of $2,000 plus $30 per day to operate. After how many days does the cost to rent equal the cost to buy?

a. 30 days
b. 40 days
c. 50 days
d. 60 days

41. A Fixed Price Incentive Fee (FPIF) Contract has the following parameters:
Target Cost = $300,000
Target Profit = $30,000
Target Price = $330,000
Ceiling Price = $375,000
Share Ratio 75/25

The project was completed for an actual cost of $390,000. What is the point of total assumption (PTA)?

a. $390,000
b. $375,000
c. $360,000
d. $325,000

42. Your organization is about to award a contract and is trying to decide between a Cost plus fixed fee (CPFF) contract and a Time and materials (T&M) contract. Which of the following is true for CPFF contracts and not true for T&M contracts?

a. The contracts can remain flexible to allow for changes due to an incomplete statement of work (SOW).
b. The seller is reimbursed for the actual legitimate labor costs.
c. The buyer often has more risk than the seller.
d. The contracts can increase in contract value.

43. A Cost Plus Incentive Fee (CPIF) Contract has the following parameters:
Target Cost = $500,000
Target Fee = $45,000
Share Ratio   50/50%
Maximum Fee = $60,000
Minimum Fee = $30,000

The seller completes the work with the buyer's permission for an actual cost of $550,000. No additional scope was added to the project. What is the final fee the seller receives?

a. $20,000
b. $30,000
c. $45,000
d. $60,000

44. From this list below the seller has the least cost risk on what contract type?

a. Cost plus incentive fee (CPIF)
b. Cost plus fixed fee (CPFF)
c. Fixed price incentive fee (FPIF)
d. Firm fixed price (FFP)

45. You have signed a cost plus fixed fee (CPFF) contract with a supplier to perform some work for you. The contract parameters include:

Estimated cost: $100,000
Fixed Fee: $10,000

The seller is able to complete the work for a cost of $80,000. What is the final price paid to the supplier?

a. $80,000
b. $90,000
c. $100,000
d. $110,000

46. Your satellite launch project has been going well. The only area that is causing issues is the cost area. The actual cost is already higher than the target cost and the project is not complete. The contract manager tells you that you are nearing the point of total assumption. This concerns both you and your management. The point of total assumption (PTA) is the point when:

a. The actual cost plus the resulting profit is equal to or greater than the price ceiling.
b. The actual cost is equal to or greater than the price ceiling.
c. The resulting profit goes to zero.
d. The seller is taking a loss.

47. A Cost Plus Incentive Fee (CPIF) Contract has the following parameters:
Target Cost = $100,000
Target Fee = $10,000
Share Ratio 70/30%
Maximum Fee = $12,000
Minimum Fee = $8,000

The seller completes the work for an actual cost of $80,000. What is the final price the seller receives?

a. $84,000
b. $88,000
c. $92,000
d. $96,000

48. Your organization is considering using a Time and materials contract (T&M) for the acquisition of outside experts. You like this contract type as it gives you, the project manager, some flexibility if you need to grow the contract. In general who has more risk under a T&M contract?

a. The buyer
b. The seller
c. The risk is shared equally
d. Neither party has much risk

49. On many contracts the buyer will audit the seller's accounting records. In fact the buyer is allowed to audit the seller's accounting records on all of the following contract types except?

a. Cost plus fixed fee (CPFF)
b. Cost plus award fee (CPAF)
c. Fixed price incentive fee (FPIF)
d. Firm fixed price (FFP)

50. Your organization sells goods and services to many non-profit organizations around the world. One of your customers is about to award a very large contract. The contract awarded will be a Cost Plus Award Fee (CPAF). You have heard that very large profits, even up to 15%, may be achieved using a CPAF. Which of the following should you be least concerned with before entering into this agreement?

a. The amount of money that could be lost on such a large project.
b. The accounting system required for accurate cost reporting.
c. The award fee is decided unilaterally by the customer.
d. The award fee criteria is often subjective.

Bonus Question 1.

You have signed a Cost plus percentage cost (CPPC) contract with a supplier to perform some work for you. The contract parameters include:

Estimated cost: $100,000
Fee Percentage: 10%.

The supplier is able to complete the work for a cost of $80,000. What is the final price paid to the supplier?

a. $80,000
b. $88,000
c. $90,000
d. $110,000

Bonus Question 2.

You have signed a Cost plus percentage cost (CPPC) contract with a supplier to perform some work for you. The contract parameters include:

Estimated cost: $100,000
Fee Percentage: 10%.

The supplier with your permission is able to complete the work for a cost of $120,000. There is no change in scope. What is the final price paid to the supplier?

a. $110,000
b. $120,000
c. $130,000
d. $132,000

Bonus Question 3.
This bonus question comes from:

You are taking over the role of project manager on a project to build a training facility for horses. Earned value management (EVM) is being used on the project and you have been handed some incomplete information. For your project, the cost performance index (CPI) = 1.2. The actual cost (AC) = $75,000. The planned value (PV) = $60,000. What is the earned value (EV) for this project?

a. $50,000
b. $62,500
c. $72,000
d. $90,000

Bonus Question 4.
This bonus question comes from:

How to get every Network Diagram Question right on the PMP®
Exam right – PMP Exam Prep Simplified Series of mini-e-books
(50+ PMP® Exam Prep Sample Questions and Solutions
on Network Diagrams, Crashing, Etc.)
(AME Group Coming late 2014)

The project schedule shows a duration of 47 weeks. After careful review management has decided that the project must finish within 42 weeks. They ask you and your team to develop a plan to crash the schedule based on cost. There are five activities on the critical path that can be crashed. Activity A has a duration of 8 weeks and can be shortened by 2 weeks for a cost of $4,000. Activity F has a duration of 9 weeks and can be shortened by 4 weeks for a cost of $16,000. Activity J has a duration of 12 weeks and can be shortened by 1 week for a cost of $2,000. Activity K has a duration of 5 weeks and can be shortened by 2 weeks for a cost of $2,000. Activity R has a duration of 8 weeks and can be shortened by 3 weeks for a cost of $9,000.
The activities that should be crashed are:

a. Activity A and Activity R
b. Activity K and Activity R
c. Activity A and Activity J and Activity K
d. Activity F and Activity J

Bonus Question 5.
This bonus question comes from:

How to get every Financial Question right on the PMP® Exam –
PMP Exam Prep Simplified Series of mini-e-books
(50+ PMP® Exam Prep Sample Questions and Solutions
on NPV, IRR, ROI, Etc.)
(AME Group Coming late 2014)

The portfolio review board is conducting a project selection review. They are going to make their decision based on the Net Present Value (NPV) estimates for the projects. The organization has only $100,000 available for investment. Based on the following information which project should they select? Assume an interest rate of 5%.

Project A - The initial investment = $100,000. The benefit at end of year one = $40,000. The additional benefit at end of year two = $70,000. There are no other benefits.

Project B – The initial investment = $100,000. There is no benefit at the end of year one. The benefit = $42,000 at end of year two. There is an additional benefit = $70,000 at end of year 3.

Which project(s) should they select?

a. Project A
b. Project B
c. Both projects since they each have a positive net present value.
d. Neither project since they each have a negative net present value.

Bonus Question 6.
This bonus question comes from:

How to get every Statistical based Question right on the PMP®
Exam – PMP Exam Prep Simplified Series of mini-e-books
(50+ PMP® Exam Prep Sample Questions and Solutions
on standard deviation, variance, probability, Etc.)
(AME Group Coming late 2014)

You are the project manager for a logging company. This month you are charted to deliver 10,000 units that are 60 centimeters each. Your upper control limit on your process is 63 centimeters. Your lower control limit on your process is 57 centimeters. Approximately what percentage of your units will be above 61 centimeters?

a. 68.3%
b. 31.7%
c. 95.5%
d. 15.9%

Part Three

1. You are trying to decide if you should rent or buy a piece of equipment for your project. The cost to rent per day is $300. The cost to purchase the piece of equipment is $14,000 plus $50 per day to operate. After how many days does the cost to rent equal the cost to buy?

a. 56 days
b. 62 days
c. 73 days
d. 84 days

Solution:
Answer (a) is the best answer.
D = the number of days when the cost to rent equals the cost to buy.
$300 * D = $14,000 + $50 * D.
Subtract ($50 * D) from each side of the equation.

$300*D -$50*D = $14,000
$250*D = $14,000
D = 56 days.

If we need the piece of equipment for more than 56 days it makes more sense to buy the equipment.
If we need the piece of equipment for less than 56 days it makes more sense to rent the equipment.

2. A Fixed Price Incentive Fee (FPIF) Contract has the following parameters:
Target Cost = $100,000
Target Profit = $10,000
Target Price = $110,000
Ceiling Price = $130,000
Share Ratio 80/20

The project was completed for an actual cost of $123,000. What is the point of total assumption (PTA)?

a. $110,000
b. $123,000
c. $125,000
d. $130,000

Solution:
Answer (c) is the best answer.
PTA = Target Cost + (Ceiling Price-Target Price)/ Buyer's Share
PTA = $100,000 + ($130,000 – $110,000) /.8
PTA = $100,000 + $20,000/.8
PTA= $125,000
The actual cost is irrelevant to solve for PTA.

3. A Cost Plus Incentive Fee (CPIF) Contract has the following parameters:
Target Cost = $300,000
Target Fee = $30,000
Share Ratio 75/25%
Maximum Fee = $45,000
Minimum Fee = $15,000

The seller completes the work with the buyer's permission for an actual cost of $320,000. No additional scope was added to the project. What is the fee the seller receives?

a. $15,000
b. $20,000
c. $25,000
d. $30,000

Solution:
Answer (c) is the best answer.
Q. What is the contract type?
Cost Plus Incentive Fee (CPIF).

Q. Do we have an over run or under run and by how much?
The target cost is $300,000.
The actual cost is $320,000.
There is an overrun of $20,000.

Q. Will the fee be increased or decreased from the target fee and by how much?
Since there is an overrun the seller's fee will decrease by the seller's percentage of the overrun. The seller's percentage is 25%.
The seller's percentage is always the second number of the share ratio.
The adjustment to the seller's fee will be 25% of $20,000.

Fee adjustment = 25% * $20,000 = $5,000.

Q. What is the actual fee?
Actual fee = target fee - fee adjustment. The $5,000 is being subtracted since there is an overrun. The seller is being penalized for the overrun.
Actual fee = Target fee - fee adjustment
Actual fee = $30,000 - $5,000
Actual fee = $25,000

Q. Is the actual fee between the minimum fee and the maximum fee?
Yes. Therefore, $25,000 is the actual fee. The actual fee must be between the minimum and the maximum fee.

4. As a buyer you would like to enter into a contract with a supplier that will entail
a tremendous amount of technical risk for the seller. You would prefer a firm fixed price contract but there is no seller willing to enter into that contract type because of the risky nature of the work. Also, the sellers who are bidding on the work are all relatively new startups without adequate accounting systems for accurate cost accounting. Most likely you will need to enter into what contract type?

a. Fixed price incentive (FPI)
b. Cost plus incentive fee (CPIF)
c. Cost plus fixed fee (CPFF)
d. Time and materials (T&M)

Solution:
Answer (d) is the best answer. As a buyer we would prefer a firm fixed price arrangement to lower our financial risk. The question states that no seller will bid under a firm fixed price arrangement. From the list, as the buyer we would prefer the fixed price incentive contract as there is less cost risk because the price ceiling protects our exposure.
The question states that the sellers do no have adequate accounting systems for accurate cost accounting. Therefore, the fixed price incentive and all cost reimbursable contracts must be ruled out as they all require the seller to accurately report on costs. By process of elimination the Time and Materials contract type is the only one left.   With a time and materials contract the seller must report on the hours (or days) spent and costs for materials. This is much easier than the reporting required on a FPI or any cost contract.

5. A Fixed Price Incentive Fee (FPIF) contract has the following parameters:
Target Cost = $200,000
Target Profit = $20,000
Target Price = $220,000
Ceiling Price = $250,000
Share Ratio 70/30

The project was completed for an actual cost of $170,000. What is the actual profit the seller receives?

a. $9,000
b. $11,000
c. $20,000
d. $29,000

Solution:
Answer (d) is the best answer.
I solve FPIF problems that ask about actual profit and/or actual price by asking and answering a set of questions:
Q. What is the contract type?
A. FPIF

Q. Do we have an over run or under run and by how much?
A. The target cost is $200,000. Make sure you always look at target cost and not target price.
The actual cost is $170,000.
There is an under run of $30,000.

Q. Will the profit be adjusted up or down and by how much?
A. Since there is an under run the seller's profit will be adjusted up by the seller's percentage of the under run. The seller's percentage is 30%.

The seller's percentage is always the second number of the share ratio.
The adjustment to the seller's profit will be 30% of $30,000.
Profit adjustment = 30% * $30,000 = $9,000.

Q. What is the actual profit?
A. Actual profit = target profit + profit adjustment.
The $9,000 is being added since there is an under run.
The seller is being rewarded for the under run.
Actual profit = $20,000 + $9,000
Actual profit = $29,000
Since there is an under run we do not need to check the actual price against the ceiling price. With an under run the actual price could never reach the ceiling price.

6. Your organization is trying to decide if you should make a purchase using a Firm fixed price (FFP) arrangement or a Cost plus fixed fee (CPFF) arrangement. Which of the following factors would make you decide to use CPFF?

a. You want the lowest risk possible for your organization.
b. You want to not have to audit the seller's accounting system.
c. You want the seller to be legally obligated under the contract to deliver with financial damages available for non-delivery.
d. You want the ability to redirect the seller because the statement of work cannot be defined in detail at the beginning of the project.

Solution:
Answer (d) is the best answer. With cost reimbursable contracts there is often flexibility to redirect the seller when the Statement of work (SOW) cannot be fully defined at the start of the contract.

Answer (a), (b), and (c) are all reasons to choose the FFP Contract. With FFP contracts the buyer has a lower risk than the seller. With a CPFF contract the buyer has a higher risk than the seller. With FFP contracts the buyer is not allowed to audit the accounting system of the seller. With the CPFF contract the buyer must audit the accounting system of the seller. With an FFP contract the seller is obligated to deliver or else there may be financial damages. With the CPFF contract the seller is obligated to make their best effort.

7. A Cost Plus Incentive Fee (CPIF) contract has the following parameters:

Target Cost = $500,000
Target Fee = $45,000
Share Ratio   50/50%
Maximum Fee = $60,000
Minimum Fee = $30,000

The seller completes the work with the buyer's permission for an actual cost of $450,000. No additional scope was added to the project. What is the final price paid that the seller receives?

a. $470,000
b. $480,000
c. $510,000
d. $520,000

Solution:
Answer (c) is the best answer.
Q. What is the contract type?
Cost Plus Incentive Fee (CPIF).

Q. Do we have an over run or under run and by how much?
The target cost is $500,000.
The actual cost is $450,000.
There is an under run of $50,000.

Q. Will the fee be increased or decreased from the target fee and by how much?
Since there is an under run the seller's fee will increase by the seller's percentage of the overrun. The seller's percentage is 50%.
The seller's percentage is always the second number of the share ratio.
The adjustment to the seller's fee will be 50% of $50,000.

Fee adjustment = 50% * $50,000 = $25,000.
Q. What is the actual fee?
Actual fee = target fee + fee adjustment. The $25,000 is being added since there is an under run. The seller is being rewarded for the under run.
Actual fee = Target fee + fee adjustment
Actual fee = $45,000 + $25,000
Actual fee = $70,000

Q. Is the actual fee between the minimum fee and the maximum fee?
No. Therefore, $70,000 cannot be the actual fee. The actual fee must be between the minimum and the maximum fee. The actual fee will be the maximum fee of $60,000.

Q. What is the actual price?
Actual price = actual cost + actual fee
Actual price = $450,000 + $60,000.
Actual price = $510,000.
Since this is a cost plus incentive fee (CPIF) contract and not a fixed price incentive fee (FPIF) contract there is no price ceiling to review.

8. Your satellite launch project has been going well. Your customer seems pleased with all areas except cost. The actual cost is already higher than the target cost and the project is not complete. The contract manager tells you that you are nearing the point of total assumption. This concerns both you and your management. The point of total assumption (PTA) is the point when:

a. Your organization takes over the entire project cost risk.
b. Your customer takes over the entire project cost risk.
c. The share ratio goes to 100/0.
d. The cost risk is equally shared between your organization and the customer organization.

Solution:
Answer (a) is the best answer. The point of total assumption (PTA) is the point when the seller (in this case your organization) assumes all the cost risk. Before this point the cost risk is shared based on the share ratio. In a FPIF contract, both the buyer and the seller share in the risk until the PTA is reached. Once the PTA is reached the share ratio goes to 0/100. This means the buyer has zero cost risk and the seller has 100% cost risk.

9. A Fixed Price Incentive Fee (FPIF) Contract has the following parameters:

Target Cost = $100,000
Target Profit = $10,000
Target Price = $110,000
Ceiling Price = $130,000
Share Ratio 80/20

The seller completes the work for an actual cost of $127,000. What is the total price paid to the seller?

a. $121,600
b. $127,000
c. $130,000
d. $131,600

Solution:
Answer (c) is the best answer.
I solve FPI problems that ask about actual profit and/or actual price by asking and answering a set of questions:

Q. What is the contract type?
A. FPI

Q. Do we have an over run or under run and by how much?
The target cost is $100,000.
The actual cost is $127,000.
There is an overrun of $27,000.

Q. Will the profit be adjusted up or down and by how much?
Since there is an overrun the seller's profit will be adjusted down by the seller's percentage of the overrun. The seller's percentage is 20%.
The seller's percentage is always the second number of the share ratio.

The adjustment to the seller's profit will be 20% of $27,000.
Profit adjustment = 20% * $27,000 = $5,400.

Q. What is the actual profit?
Actual profit = target profit - profit adjustment. The $5,400 is being subtracted since there is an overrun. The seller is being penalized for the overrun.
Actual profit = $10,000 - $5,400
Actual profit = $4,600

The question is asking for the actual price.
Q. What is the actual price?
Actual price = actual cost + actual profit
Actual price = $127,000 + $4,600
Actual price = $131,600

Q. Is the actual price above or below the ceiling?
A. Above. The actual price can never be higher than the ceiling price.
The actual price therefore will be the ceiling price if $130,000. Since the actual cost is $127,000 the profit really is $3,000.

10. We are entering into a long-term contract with a supplier. There are multiple commodity type items that will be delivered as part of this contract. We want a contract type where we can precisely adjust the final price based on an outside financial index. What contract type are we most likely to use?

a. Firm fixed price (FFP)
b. Fixed price incentive fee (FPIF)
c. Fixed price with economic price adjustment (FP-EPA)
d. Cost plus incentive fee (CPIF)

Solution:
Answer (c) is the best answer. FP-EPA contracts are often used when we want to be able to adjust the final price based on an external reliable financial index. We see the use of these contracts for long-term work. Often we use them when there are commodities as part of the contract whose cost is likely to change over the life of the contract. At other times these contracts are used to help deal with inflation changes.

11. A Fixed Price Incentive Fee (FPIF) Contract has the following parameters:
Target Cost = $200,000
Target Profit = $20,000
Target Price = $220,000
Ceiling Price = $250,000
Share Ratio 70/30

The project was completed for an actual cost of $218,576. What is the point of total assumption (PTA)?

a. $238,576
b. $222,857
c. $262,857
d. $242,857

Solution:
Answer (d) is the best answer.
PTA = Target Cost + (Ceiling Price-Target Price)/ Buyer's Share
PTA = $200,000 + ($250,000 – $220,000) /.7
PTA = $200,000 + $30,000/.7
PTA = $200,000 + $42,857
PTA = $242,857
The actual cost is irrelevant to solve for PTA.

12. As a buyer you are trying to enter into a contract relationship with a low cost risk. The most likely contract type you will use is:

a. Time and materials (T&M)
b. Cost plus fixed fee (CPFF)
c. Cost plus incentive fee (CPIF)
d. Firm fixed price (FFP)

Solution:
Answer (d) is the best answer. As a buyer the firm fixed price (FFP) contract type has the least financial risk for you. With the FFP contract type your cost risk exposure is low since you only will make payment if the seller can meet your requirements. You should realize this is the highest cost risk contract type for the seller.

13. A Cost Plus Incentive Fee (CPIF) Contract has the following parameters:

Target Cost = $600,000
Target Fee = $60,000
Share Ratio 80/20%
Maximum Fee = $80,000
Minimum Fee = $40,000

The seller completes the work for an actual cost of $630,000. What is the total price the seller receives?

a. $720,000
b. $600,000
c. $696,000
d. $684,000

Solution:
Answer (d) is the best answer.

Q. What is the contract type?
A. Cost Plus Incentive Fee (CPIF)

Q. Do we have an over run or under run and by how much?
The target cost is $60,000
The actual cost is $630,000
There is an overrun of $30,000

Q. Will the fee be increased or decreased from the target fee and by how much?
Since there is an overrun the seller's fee will decrease by the seller's percentage of the overrun. The seller's percentage is 20%.
The seller's percentage is always the second number of the share ratio.
The adjustment to the seller's fee will be 20% of $30,000.

Fee adjustment = 20% * $30,000 = $6,000
Q. What is the actual fee?
Actual fee = target fee - fee adjustment. The $6,000 is being subtracted since there is an overrun. The seller is being penalized for the overrun.
Actual fee = Target fee - fee adjustment
Actual fee = $60,000 - $6,000
Actual fee = $54,000

Q. Is the actual fee between the minimum fee and the maximum fee?
Yes. Therefore, $54,000 is the actual fee. The actual fee must be between the minimum and the maximum fee.

Q. What is the actual price?
Actual price = actual cost + actual fee
Actual price = $630,000 + $54,000.
Actual price = $684,000.

14. You are trying to decide if you should lease or purchase a piece of equipment for your project. The daily lease cost is $50. To purchase the equipment will require an investment of $3,000 plus $20 per day to operate. After how many days does the cost to lease equal the cost to purchase?

a. 30 days
b. 50 days
c. 70 days
d. 100 days

Solution:
Answer (d) is the best answer.
D = The number of days when the cost to rent equals the cost to buy.

$50 * D = $3,000 + $20 * D
Subtract ($20 * D) from each side of the equation.

$50*D - 20*D = $3,000
$30*D = $3,000
D = 100 days.

If we need the piece of equipment for more than 100 days it makes more sense to purchase the equipment. If we need the piece of equipment for less than 100 days it makes more sense to lease the equipment.

15. A Fixed Price Incentive Fee (FPIF) Contract has the following parameters:

Target Cost = $200,000
Target Profit = $20,000
Target Price = $220,000
Ceiling Price = $250,000
Share Ratio 70/30

The project was completed for an actual cost of $150,000. What is the actual profit the seller receives?

a. $35,000
b. $20,000
c. $15,000
d. $10,000

Solution:
Answer (a) is the best answer.
I solve FPI problems that ask about actual profit and/or actual price by asking and answering a set of questions:
Q. What is the contract type?
FPI

Q. Do we have an over run or under run and by how much?
The target cost is $200,000.
The actual cost is $150,000.
There is an under run of $50,000.

Q. Will the profit be adjusted up or down and by how much?
Since there is an under run the seller's profit will be adjusted up by the seller's percentage of the under run. The seller's percentage is 30%.
The seller's percentage is always the second number of the share ratio.

The adjustment to the seller's profit will be 30% of $50,000.
Profit adjustment = 30% * $50,000 = $15,000.

Q. What is the actual profit?
Actual profit = target profit + profit adjustment. The $9,000 is being added since there is an under run. The seller is being rewarded for the under run.
Actual profit = $20,000 + $15,000
Actual profit = $35,000
Since there is an under run we do not need to check the actual price against the ceiling price. With an under run the actual price could never reach the ceiling price.

16. Your organization is entering into a Cost plus fixed fee (CPFF) contract with a new supplier. You are trying to explain how the fixed fee is developed. The best way to describe this is:

a. The fixed fee is a percentage of the actual costs.
b. The fixed fee is a percentage of the actual costs plus the actual profits.
c. The fixed fee is a percentage of the estimated costs.
d. The fixed fee is a percentage of the estimated costs plus the estimated profits.

Solution:
Answer (c) is the best answer.
Before the contract is signed, the buyer and the seller agree on the estimated costs. The estimated costs are what the buyer and the seller believe it will cost the seller to complete the work. The buyer and seller will then look at the nature of the work as well as other parameters to determine a reasonable fee. Fee means profit. This fee is a percentage of the estimated costs. This fee now changes from a percentage of the estimated costs to a fixed number. The fixed fee is the profit paid to the supplier. It does not change, regardless of the seller's actual costs unless there is a change in scope.

Let's take a look at an example.
The buyer and seller agree that the estimated cost for a project is $100. Based on the nature of the work they agree that the seller should receive a 10% fee (meaning profit) for the work. 10% of $100 = $10. The $10 now becomes the fixed fee. It is no longer a percentage. The seller completes the work for an actual cost of $80. The seller receives $10 in fee. The seller does not receive 10% of the actual cost of $80.

17. A Cost Plus Incentive Fee (CPIF) Contract has the following parameters:
Target Cost = $96,000
Target Fee = $6,000
Share Ratio 90/10%
Maximum Fee = $8,000
Minimum Fee = $4,000

The seller completes the work for an actual cost of $86,000. What is the fee the seller receives?

a. $4,000
b. $5,000
c. $7,000
d. $8,000

Solution:
Answer (c) is the best answer.

Q. What is the contract type?
Cost Plus Incentive Fee (CPIF).

Q. Do we have an over run or under run and by how much?
The target cost is $96,000.
The actual cost is $86,000.
There is an under run of $10,000.

Q. Will the fee be increased or decreased from the target fee and by how much?
Since there is an under run the seller's fee will increase by the seller's percentage of the under run. The seller's percentage is 10%.
The seller's percentage is always the second number of the share ratio.
The adjustment to the seller's fee will be 10% of $10,000.
Fee adjustment = 10% * $10,000 = $1,000.

Q. What is the actual fee?
Actual fee = target fee + fee adjustment. The $1,000 is being added since there is an under run. The seller is being rewarded for the under run.
Actual fee = Target fee + fee adjustment
Actual fee = $6,000 + $1,000
Actual fee = $7,000

Q. Is the actual fee between the minimum fee and the maximum fee?
Yes. Therefore, $7,000 is the actual fee. The actual fee must be between the minimum and the maximum fee.

18. You have signed a cost plus fixed fee (CPFF) with a supplier to perform some work for you. The contract parameters include:

Estimated cost: $100,000
Fixed Fee: $10,000.

The seller is able to complete the work for a cost of $120,000. The supplier had your permission to spend this amount of money. There is no change in scope. What is the final price paid to the supplier?

a. $100,000
b. $130,000
c. $132,000
d. $133,000

Solution:
Answer (b) is the best answer.

Actual price = actual cost + fixed fee.
Actual price = $120,000 + $10,000
Actual price = $130,000.
The fixed fee is fixed if the seller is able to complete the work. Be sure to think of the fixed fee as a fixed amount and not a fixed percentage.

19. A Fixed Price Incentive Fee (FPIF) contract has the following parameters:
Target Cost = $100,000
Target Profit = $10,000
Target Price = $110,000
Ceiling Price = $130,000
Share Ratio 80/20

The seller completes the work for an actual cost of $128,000. What is the actual profit paid to the seller?

a. $0
b. $2,000
c. $4,400
d. $5,600

Solution:
Answer (b) is the best answer.

I solve FPI problems that ask about actual profit and/or actual price by asking and answering a set of questions:

Q. What is the contract type?
A. FPI

Q. Do we have an over run or under run and by how much?
The target cost is $100,000.
The actual cost is $128,000.
There is an overrun of $28,000.

Q. Will the profit be adjusted up or down and by how much?
Since there is an overrun the seller's profit will be adjusted down by the seller's percentage of the overrun. The seller's percentage is 20%.

The seller's percentage is always the second number of the share ratio.

The adjustment to the seller's profit will be 20% of $28,000.

Profit adjustment = 20% * $28,000 = $5,600.

Q. What is the actual profit?

Actual profit = target profit - profit adjustment. The $5,600 is being subtracted since there is an overrun. The seller is being penalized for the overrun.

Actual profit = $10,000 - $5,600

Actual profit = $4,400.

Since there is an overrun we cannot stop here. We must check the actual price to see if we have reached the price ceiling.

Q. What is the actual price?

Actual price = actual cost + actual profit

Actual price = $128,000 + $4,400

Actual price = $132,400

Q. Is the actual price above or below the ceiling?

Above. The actual price can never be higher than the ceiling price.

The actual price therefore will be the ceiling price if $130,000.

Since the actual cost is $128,000 the profit really is $2,000.

20. You are about to award a contract to a seller who will provide long-term product development and testing for a period of four years. Your organization is trying to decide between a Fixed Price Incentive Fee (FPIF) and a Cost Plus Incentive Fee (CPIF) contract. Which of the following is the major difference that separates a FPIF from a CPIF?

a. When the seller overruns the seller's profit is decreased.
b. When the seller under runs the seller's profit is increased.
c. There is a price ceiling to protect the buyer.
d. There is a share ratio that represents how the buyer and seller will share cost overruns and under runs.

Solution:
Answer (c) is the best answer.
FPIF contracts have a ceiling price. A CPIF contract does not have a ceiling price.
The other three answers are true for both FPIF and CPIF contracts.

21. A Fixed Price Incentive Fee (FPIF) Contract has the following parameters:

Target Cost = $1,000,000
Target Profit = $87,500
Target Price = $1,087,500
Ceiling Price = $1,150,000
Share Ratio 70/30

What is the point of total assumption (PTA)?

a. $1,089,286
b. $1,087,500
c. $1,031,242
d. $985,326

Solution:
Answer (a) is the best answer.
PTA = Target Cost + (Ceiling Price-Target Price)/ Buyer's Share
PTA = $1,000,000 + (1,150,000 – 1,087,500) /.7
PTA = $1,000,000 + $62.500/.7
PTA = $1.000.000 + $89,286
PTA = $1,089,286

22. Your organization is making a large purchase. Your goal is to build a strong long-term relationship with the seller. It is imperative for the success of the project for the two organizations to work well together. You would like to provide incentives to the seller and at times these incentives will need to be quite subjective. You decide to set up a contract type that will ensure the seller's objectives are completely aligned with your objectives. The most likely contract type to do this is:

a. Cost plus award fee (CPAF)
b. Time and materials (T&M)
c. Fixed price incentive (FPI)
d. Cost plus incentive fee (CPIF)

Solution:
Answer (a) is the best answer.
With a cost plus award fee contract (CPAF) the fee pool is managed by an award fee plan. The award fee plan will include the subjective criteria as well as many other items related to the award fee. The true goal of a CPAF is for the seller's objectives to be completely aligned with the buyer's objectives. The FPI and the CPIF both have very objective, not subjective incentives. There are no incentives in a pure T&M contract.

23. A Cost Plus Incentive Fee (CPIF) Contract has the following parameters:
Target Cost = $100,000
Target Fee = $10,000
Share Ratio 70/30%
Maximum Fee = $12,000
Minimum Fee = $8,000

The seller completes the work with the buyer's permission for an actual cost of $120,000. No additional scope was added to the project. What is the fee the seller receives?

a. $4,000
b. $8,000
c. $10,000
d. $16,000

Solution:
Answer (b) is the best answer.
Q. What is the contract type?
Cost Plus Incentive Fee (CPIF).

Q. Do we have an over run or under run and by how much?
The target cost is $100,000.
The actual cost is $120,000.
There is an overrun of $20,000.

Q. Will the fee be increased or decreased from the target fee and by how much?
Since there is an overrun the seller's fee will decrease by the seller's percentage of the overrun. The seller's percentage is 30%.
The seller's percentage is always the second number of the share ratio.
The adjustment to the seller's fee will be 30% of $20,000.

Fee adjustment = 30% * $20,000 = $6,000.
Q. What is the actual fee?
Actual fee = target fee - fee adjustment. The $6,000 is being subtracted since there is an overrun. The seller is being penalized for the overrun.
Actual fee = Target fee - fee adjustment
Actual fee = $10,000 - $6,000
Actual fee = $4,000

Q. Is the actual fee between the minimum fee and the maximum fee?
No. Therefore, $4,000 cannot be the actual fee. The actual fee must be between the minimum and the maximum fee.
The actual fee will be the minimum fee of $8,000.

24. You are the project manager for an organization selling products and services to many different customers. In some contract types it is more important than others to have a clear definition of scope. Which contract type are you least likely to enter if you have concerns about an unclear scope definition?

a. **Time and materials**
b. **Cost plus fixed fee**
c. **Cost plus incentive cost**
d. **Firm fixed price**

Solution:
Answer (d) is the best answer.
As a seller we have the most concerns about a clear scope definition in a Firm fixed price (FFP) contract. With the FFP contract we as the seller should not be paid unless we meet the contract requirements. Therefore, we want the contract requirements to be very clear.

25. A Fixed Price Incentive Fee (FPIF) Contract has the following parameters:
Target Cost = $100,000
Target Profit = $10,000
Target Price = $110,000
Ceiling Price = $130,000
Share Ratio 80/20

The seller completes the work for an actual cost of $90,000. What is the profit paid to the seller?

a. $2,000
b. $10,000
c. $12,000
d. $14,000

Solution:
Answer (c) is the best answer.
I solve FPI problems that ask about actual profit and/or actual price by asking and answering a set of questions:
Q. What is the contract type?
  FPI

Q. Do we have an over run or under run and by how much?
The target cost is $100,000.
The actual cost is $90,000.
There is an under run of $10,000.

Q. Will the profit be adjusted up or down and by how much?
Since there is an under run the seller's profit will be adjusted up by the seller's percentage of the under run. The seller's percentage is 20%.
The seller's percentage is always the second number of the share ratio.

The adjustment to the seller's profit will be 20% of $10,000.

Profit adjustment = 20% * $10,000 = $2,000.

Q. What is the actual profit?

Actual profit = target profit + profit adjustment. The $2,000 is being added since there is an under run. The seller is being rewarded for the under run.

Actual profit = $10,000 + $2,000

Actual profit = $12,000

Since there is an under run we do not need to check the actual price against the ceiling price. With an under run the actual price could never reach the ceiling price.

26. You are trying to decide if you should rent or buy a piece of equipment for your project. The daily cost to rent is $115. To buy the equipment will require an investment of $4,000 plus $35 per day to operate. After how many days does the cost to rent equal the cost to buy?

a. 30 days
b. 40 days
c. 50 days
d. 60 days

Solution:
Answer (c) is the best answer.
D = the number of days when the cost to rent equals the cost to buy.

$115*D = $4,000 + $35*D
Subtract ($35*D) from each side of the equation.

$115*D - $35*D = $4,000
$80*D = $4,000
D = 50 days.

If we need the piece of equipment for more than 50 days it makes more sense to buy the equipment.
If we need the piece of equipment for less than 50 days it makes more sense to rent the equipment.

27. A Cost Plus Incentive Fee (CPIF) Contract has the following parameters:
Target Cost = $300,000
Target Fee = $30,000
Share Ratio 75/25%
Maximum Fee = $45,000
Minimum Fee = $15,000

The seller completes the work for an actual cost of $280,000. What is the final price the seller receives?

a. $295,000
b. $315,000
c. $325,000
d. $335,000

Solution:
Answer (b) is the best answer.

Q. What is the contract type?
Cost Plus Incentive Fee (CPIF).

Q. Do we have an overrun or under run and by how much?
The target cost is $300,000.
The actual cost is $280,000.
There is an under run of $20,000.

Q. Will the fee be increased or decreased from the target fee and by how much?
Since there is an overrun the seller's fee will be increased by the seller's percentage of the under run.
The seller's percentage is 25%.
The seller's percentage is always the second number of the share ratio.
The adjustment to the seller's fee will be 25% of $20,000.
Fee adjustment = 25% * $20,000 = $5,000.

Q. What is the actual fee?
Actual fee = target fee + fee adjustment. The $5,000 is being added since there is an under run. The seller is being rewarded for the under run.
Actual fee = Target fee + fee adjustment
Actual fee = $30,000 + $5,000
Actual fee = $35,000

Q. Is the actual fee between the minimum fee and the maximum fee?
Yes. Therefore, $35,000 is the actual fee. The actual fee must be between the minimum and the maximum fee.

Q. What is the actual price?
Actual price = actual cost + actual fee
Actual price = $280,000 + $35,000.
Actual price = $315,000.
Since this is a cost plus incentive fee (CPIF) contract and not a fixed price incentive fee (FPIF) contract there is no price ceiling to review.

28. We are about to enter into a contract with a long-term supplier. Over the last several years the relationship with the supplier has been very positive. Because of this history we are entering into a contract that will span ten years. This represents the longest commitment our organization has ever made to a supplier. As we move forward with the contract we see tremendous market instability. There seems to be uncertainty for not just material costs but also for labor costs. Most likely we will enter into what type of contract?

a. Firm fixed price (FFP)
b. Cost plus percentage cost (CPPC)
c. Time and materials (T&M)
d. Fixed price with economic price adjustment (FP-EPA)

Solution:
Answer (d) is the best answer.
There are several hints in this question that bring us to the FP-EPA. One hint is the length of the contract. Often with contracts for long periods of time, such as ten years, you should provide for certain adjustments based on specific contingencies. Another hint in the question is the term "tremendous market instability." If the market is unstable and the contract is for a long period of time there needs to be a way to adjust the final contract price to protect both the buyer and the seller. A third hint is the phrase " uncertainty for not just material costs but also for labor costs." This hint tells us we need an adjustable contract type.

29. A Fixed Price Incentive Fee (FPIF) contract has the following parameters:
Target Cost = $200,000
Target Profit = $20,000
Target Price = $220,000
Ceiling Price = $250,000
Share Ratio 70/30

The seller completes the work for an actual cost of $240,000. What is the actual price paid to the seller?

a. $248,000
b. $250,000
c. $252,000
d. $272,000

Solution:
Answer (a) is the best answer.

I solve FPI problems that ask about actual profit and/or actual price by asking and answering a set of questions:
Q. What is the contract type?
A. FPI

Q. Do we have an over run or under run and by how much?
The target cost is $200,000.
The actual cost is $240,000.
There is an overrun of $40,000.

Q. Will the profit be adjusted up or down and by how much?
Since there is an overrun the seller's profit will be adjusted down by the seller's percentage of the overrun. The seller's percentage is 30%.

The seller's percentage is always the second number of the share ratio.
The adjustment to the seller's profit will be 30% of $40,000.
Profit adjustment = 30% * $40,000 = $12,000.

Q. What is the actual profit?
Actual profit = target profit - profit adjustment. The $12,000 is being subtracted since there is an overrun. The seller is being penalized for the overrun.
Actual profit = $20,000 - $12,000
Actual profit = $8,000.

Q. What is the actual price?
Actual price = actual cost + actual profit
Actual price = $240,00 + $8,000
Actual price = $248,000

Q. Is the actual price above or below the ceiling?
Lower. The actual price can never be higher than the ceiling price.
$248,000 is lower than the ceiling price of $250,000.
The actual price is $248,000.

30. Of the following contract types which one in general has the highest risk for the seller?

a. Firm fixed price (FFP)
b. Time and materials (T&M)
c. Cost plus fixed fee (CPFF)
d. Cost plus incentive fee (CPIF)

Solution:
Answer (a) is the best answer.
In general the FFP contract type is a higher risk for the seller and a lower risk for the buyer. In an FFP the seller must be able to meet the requirements to be paid. In the other contracts listed the seller must put forth their best effort to be paid.

31. A Fixed Price Incentive Contract has the following parameters:
Target Cost = $400,000
Target Profit = $40,000
Target Price = $440,000
Ceiling Price = $500,000
Share Ratio 80/20

The project was completed for an actual cost of $442,183. What is the point of total assumption (PTA)?

a. $475,000
b. $442,183
c. $425,000
d. $415,000

Solution:
Answer (a) is the best answer.
PTA = Target Cost + (Ceiling Price-Target Price)/ Buyer's Share
PTA = $400,000 + ($500,000 – $440,000) /.8
PTA = $400,000 + $60,000/.8
PTA = $400,000 + $75,000
PTA = $475,000
The actual cost is irrelevant to solve for PTA.

32. You are the project manager overseeing the transfer of technology into a new factory. The project is going well yet you underestimated the need for the specific labor of electricians and plumbers. You will need to augment your staff for several weeks to fill the gaps. At this point it is unclear exactly what work this specific labor will perform and exactly how much time you will need from them. Most likely you will use what contract type?

a. Firm fixed price
b. Fixed price incentive
c. Cost plus fixed fee
d. Time and materials

Solution:
Answer (d) is the best answer. There are several hints in the question that bring us to T&M. The phrase "augment staff" is often associated with T&M. T&M contracts are relatively easy to set up and easy to stop. They have clear advantages for short-term work when it is hard to estimate the exact amount or type of work to be performed.

33. A Cost Plus Incentive Fee (CPIF) Contract has the following parameters:
Target Cost = $96,000
Target Fee = $6,000
Share Ratio 90/10
Maximum Fee = $8,000
Minimum Fee = $4,000

The seller completes the work with the buyer's permission for an actual cost of $106,000. No additional scope was added to the project. What is the final price the seller receives?

a. $100,000
b. $104,000
c. $111,000
d. $113,000

Solution:
Answer (c) is the best answer.
Q. What is the contract type?
Cost Plus Incentive Fee (CPIF).

Q. Do we have an over run or under run and by how much?
The target cost is $96,000.
The actual cost is $106,000.
There is an overrun of $10,000.

Q. Will the fee be increased or decreased from the target fee and by how much?
Since there is an overrun the seller's fee will decrease by the seller's percentage of the overrun. The seller's percentage is 10%.
The seller's percentage is always the second number of the share ratio.
The adjustment to the seller's fee will be 10% of $10,000.

Fee adjustment = 10% * $10,000 = $1,000.

Q. What is the actual fee?
Actual fee = target fee - fee adjustment. The $1,000 is being subtracted since there is an overrun. The seller is being penalized for the overrun.
Actual fee = Target fee - fee adjustment
Actual fee = $6,000 - $1,000
Actual fee = $5,000

Q. Is the actual fee between the minimum fee and the maximum fee?
Yes. Therefore, $5,000 is the actual fee. The actual fee must be between the minimum and the maximum fee.

Q. What is the actual price?
Actual price = actual cost + actual fee
Actual price = $106,000 + $5,000.
Actual price = $111,000.

34. Your organization is about to award a contract and is trying to decide between a Cost plus award fee (CPAF) contract and a Cost plus incentive fee (CPIF) contract. Which of the following is true for the CPAF but not true for the CPIF?

a. The fee is based on broad subjective performance criteria.
b. The seller is reimbursed for all legitimate costs.
c. The buyer has flexibility to redirect the seller if the original statement of work was not clearly defined.
d. The seller is required to put forth their best effort to get reimbursed.

Solution:
Answer (a) is the best answer.
In a CPAF the award fee is based on achieving certain broad subjective performance criteria. In a CPIF the incentive fee is based on achieving certain clear objective performance criteria.
Answer (b), (c), and (d) are true for both the CPAF and the CPIF.

35. A Fixed Price Incentive Fee (FPIF) contract has the following parameters:
Target Cost = $100,000
Target Profit = $10,000
Target Price = $110,000
Ceiling Price = $130,000
Share Ratio 80/20

The seller completes the work for an actual cost of $80,000. What is the total price paid to the seller?

a. $80,000
b. $90,000
c. $94,000
d. $96,000

Solution:
Answer (c) is the best answer.

I solve FPI problems that ask about actual profit and/or actual price by asking and answering a set of questions:
Q. What is the contract type?
A. FPI

Q. Do we have an over run or under run and by how much?
The target cost is $100,000.
The actual cost is $80,000.
There is an under run of $20,000.

Q. Will the profit be adjusted up or down and by how much?
Since there is an under run the seller's profit will be adjusted up by the seller's percentage of the under run. The seller's percentage is 20%.
The seller's percentage is always the second number of the share ratio.

The adjustment to the seller's profit will be 20% of $20,000.
Profit adjustment = 20% * $20,000 = 4,000.

Q. What is the actual profit?
Actual profit = target profit + profit adjustment. The $4,000 is being added since there is an under run. The seller is being rewarded for the under run.
Actual profit = $10,000 + $4,000
Actual profit = $14,000

The question is asking for the actual price.
Q. What is the actual price?
Actual price = actual cost + actual profit
Actual price = $80,000 + $14,000
Actual price = $94,000
Since there is an under run we do not need to check the actual price against the ceiling price. With an under run the actual price could never reach the ceiling price.

36. You are the project manager for a large government agency. Your organization requires a supplier to perform long-term research and development. You truly want the contractor to focus on the nature of the work and not be concerned with incentives. Most likely you will want what contract type?

a. Firm fixed price (FFP)
b. Cost plus award fee (CPAF)
c. Cost plus fixed fee (CPFF)
d. Time and materials (T&M)

Solution:
Answer (c) is the best answer.
Research and development is almost never performed under a FFP contract. Under a FFP contract the seller is not paid unless they can meet the requirements. A seller may not be able to meet the requirements while performing research and development. The question states that we do not want the seller concerned with incentives. Therefore, CPAF is eliminated because there is so much focus on incentives in this contract type. Answer (c) is absolutely the best answer. With a CPFF the seller is reimbursed for all reasonable costs plus they are guaranteed a fee on top of the costs. T&M is more often used for short-term, not long-term work.

37. A Cost Plus Incentive Fee (CPIF) Contract has the following parameters:
Target Cost = $600,000
Target Fee = $60,000
Share Ratio 80/20%
Maximum Fee = $65,000
Minimum Fee = $55,000

The seller completes the work for an actual cost of $570,000. What is the actual fee the seller receives?

a. $54,000
b. $55,000
c. $65,000
d. $66,000

Solution:
Answer (c) is the best answer.
Q. What is the contract type?
A. Cost Plus Incentive Fee (CPIF)

Q. Do we have an over run or under run and by how much?
The target cost is $60,000
The actual cost is $570,000
There is an under run of $30,000

Q. Will the fee be increased or decreased from the target fee and by how much?
Since there is an under run the seller's fee will increase by the seller's percentage of the under run. The seller's percentage is 20%.
The seller's percentage is always the second number of the share ratio.
The adjustment to the seller's fee will be 20% of $30,000
Fee adjustment = 20% * $30,000 = $6,000

Q. What is the actual fee?
Actual fee = target fee + fee adjustment. The $6,000 is being added since there is an under run. The seller is being rewarded for the under run.
Actual fee = Target fee + fee adjustment
Actual fee = $60,000 + $6,000
Actual fee = $66,000

Q. Is the actual fee between the minimum fee and the maximum fee?
No. Therefore, $66,000 cannot be the actual fee. The actual fee must be between the minimum and the maximum fee. The actual fee will be the maximum fee of $65,000.

38. Of the following contract types which one in general has the lowest risk for the seller?

a. **Firm fixed price (FFP)**
b. **Cost plus percentage cost (CPPC)**
c. **Cost plus fixed fee (CPFF)**
d. **Cost plus incentive fee (CPIF)**

Solution:
Answer (b) is the best answer. It is hard to know if CPPC contracts will be covered on the PMP® exam since they are not covered in the PMBOK Guide®.
With a CPPC there is a reverse incentive. The more the seller overruns the larger the profit gets. This is low risk for the seller.
If CPPC was not on this list then the CPFF would be the least risky for the seller. In a CPFF the seller's legitimate costs are covered plus they receive a fee. In this context fee mean profit. From this list the FFP provides the most risk for the seller. A seller must deliver under a FFP to receive payment.

39. A Fixed Price Incentive Fee (FPIF) contract has the following parameters:
Target Cost = $200,000
Target Profit = $20,000
Target Price = $220,000
Ceiling Price = $250,000
Share Ratio 70/30

The seller completes the work for an actual cost of $245,000. What is the actual profit paid to the seller?

a. $5,000
b. $6,500
c. $13,500
d. $33,500

Solution:
Answer (a) is the best answer.
I solve FPI problems that ask about actual profit and/or actual price by asking and answering a set of questions:
Q. What is the contract type?
A. FPI

Q. Do we have an over run or under run and by how much?
The target cost is $200,000.
The actual cost is $245,000.
There is an overrun of $45,000.

Q. Will the profit be adjusted up or down and by how much?
Since there is an overrun the seller's profit will be adjusted down by the seller's percentage of the overrun. The seller's percentage is 30%.

The seller's percentage is always the second number of the share ratio.
The adjustment to the seller's profit will be 30% of $45,000.
Profit adjustment = 30% * $45,000 = $13,500.

Q. What is the actual profit?
Actual profit = target profit - profit adjustment. The $13,500 is being subtracted since there is an overrun. The seller is being penalized for the overrun.
Actual profit = $20,000 - $13,500
Actual profit = $6,500.

Since there is an overrun we cannot stop here. We must check the actual price to see if we have reached the price ceiling.

Q. What is the actual price?
Actual price = actual cost + actual profit
Actual price = $245,000 + $6,500
Actual price = $251,500

Q. Is the actual price above or below the ceiling?
The actual price can never be higher than the ceiling price.
$251,500 is higher than the ceiling price of $250,000. Therefore, the actual price is $250,000.

Q. What is really the actual profit?
If the actual price is $250,000 and the actual cost is $245,000 the actual profit is $5,000.
Actual price = actual cost + actual profit
Actual price - actual cost = actual profit
$250,000 - $245,000 = actual profit.
Actual profit = $5,000

40. You are trying to decide if you should rent or buy a piece of equipment for your project. The daily cost to rent is $80. To buy the equipment will require an investment of $2,000 plus $30 per day to operate. After how many days does the cost to rent equal the cost to buy?

a. 30 days
b. 40 days
c. 50 days
d. 60 days

Solution:
Answer (b) is the best answer.
D = the number of days when the cost to rent equals the cost to buy.

$80*D = $2,000 + $30*D
Subtract ($30*D) from each side of the equation.

$80*D - $30*D = $2,000
$50*D = $2,000
D = 40 days.

If we need the piece of equipment for more than 40 days it makes more sense to buy the equipment.
If we need the piece of equipment for less than 40 days it makes more sense to rent the equipment.

41. A Fixed Price Incentive Fee (FPIF) Contract has the following parameters:

Target Cost = $300,000
Target Profit = $30,000
Target Price = $330,000
Ceiling Price = $375,000
Share Ratio 75/25

The project was completed for an actual cost of $390,000. What is the point of total assumption (PTA)?

a. $390,000
b. $375,000
c. $360,000
d. $325,000

Solution:
Answer (c) is the best answer.
PTA = Target Cost + (Ceiling Price - Target Price)/ Buyer's Share
PTA = $300,000 + ($375,000 – $330,000) /.75
PTA = $300,000 + $45,000/.75
PTA = $300,000 + $60,000
PTA = $360,000
The actual cost is irrelevant to solve for PTA.

42. Your organization is about to award a contract and is trying to decide between a Cost plus fixed fee (CPFF) contract and a Time and materials (T&M) contract. Which of the following is true for CPFF contracts and not true for T&M contracts?

a. The contracts can remain flexible to allow for changes due to an incomplete statement of work (SOW).
b. The seller is reimbursed for the actual legitimate labor costs.
c. The buyer often has more risk than the seller.
d. The contracts can increase in contract value.

Solution:
Answer (b) is the best answer. On a CPFF the seller is reimbursed for the actual legitimate labor costs. On a T&M the seller is reimbursed for the labor rate that was agreed to in the contract. The rate may or may not reflect actual legitimate labor costs.
Answers (a), (c), and (d) are true for both CPFF and the T&M contracts.

43. A Cost Plus Incentive Fee (CPIF) Contract has the following parameters:
Target Cost = $500,000
Target Fee = $45,000
Share Ratio   50/50%
Maximum Fee = $60,000
Minimum Fee = $30,000

The seller completes the work with the buyer's permission for an actual cost of $550,000. No additional scope was added to the project. What is the final fee the seller receives?

a. $20,000
b. $30,000
c. $45,000
d. $60,000

Solution:
Answer (b) is the best answer.
Q. What is the contract type?
Cost Plus Incentive Fee (CPIF).

Q. Do we have an over run or under run and by how much?
The target cost is $500,000.
The actual cost is $550,000.
There is an overrun of $50,000.

Q. Will the fee be increased or decreased from the target fee and by how much?
Since there is an overrun the seller's fee will decrease by the seller's percentage of the overrun. The seller's percentage is 50%.
The seller's percentage is always the second number of the share ratio.
The adjustment to the seller's fee will be 50% of $50,000.

Fee adjustment = 50% * $50,000 = $25,000.
Q. What is the actual fee?
Actual fee = target fee - fee adjustment. The $25,000 is being subtracted since there is an overrun. The seller is being penalized for the overrun.
Actual fee = Target fee - fee adjustment
Actual fee = $45,000 - $25,000
Actual fee = $20,000

Q. Is the actual fee between the minimum fee and the maximum fee?
No. Therefore, $20,000 cannot be the actual fee. The actual fee must be between the minimum and the maximum fee. The actual fee is the minimum fee of $30,000.

44. From this list below the seller has the least cost risk on what contract type?

a. **Cost plus incentive fee (CPIF)**
b. **Cost plus fixed fee (CPFF)**
c. **Fixed price incentive fee (FPIF)**
d. **Firm fixed price (FFP)**

Solution:
Answer (b) is the best answer from this list.
To put these contract types in order from least to most risk for the seller the list would be:
CPFF
CPIF
FPIF
FFP

The risky situation for the seller is if there is an overrun.
With the CPFF the seller receives a fixed fee for completing the work regardless if there is an overrun or under run. This is low risk for the seller as they receive the same fixed fee regardless of the size of their overrun, as long as the spending is approved.

On a CPIF the seller may receive a higher fee if there is an under run but may receive a lower fee if there is an overrun. Therefore, the CPIF is more risky for the seller than the CPFF.

On a FPIF the seller may receive a higher fee if there is an under run but may receive a lower fee if there is an overrun. With an extreme overrun the seller may reach the PTA (point of total assumption). At this point the seller assumes all the cost risk. If the overrun gets worse the seller may reach the ceiling price. At this point the seller will begin to take a loss on the contract. Therefore, the FPIF is more risky for the seller than the CPFF.

On a FFP the seller may take a loss if his costs are greater than the contract price.

There is a contract type that is even less risker for the seller than the CPFF. The least risky contract for the seller is CPPC. I have not put the CPPC on the list because I am unsure if the CPPC will be discussed on the PMP® Exam. The CPPC would be of less risk for the seller than the CPFF. On a CPPC the fee continues to grow as the overrun grows. This is good for the seller and bad for the buyer. On a CPFF the fee is fixed regardless of the value of the overrun. This is bad for the seller and good for the buyer.

45. You have signed a cost plus fixed fee (CPFF) contract with a supplier to perform some work for you. The contract parameters include:

Estimated cost: $100,000
Fixed Fee: $10,000

The seller is able to complete the work for a cost of $80,000. What is the final price paid to the supplier?

a. $80,000
b. $90,000
c. $100,000
d. $110,000

Solution:
Answer (b) is the best answer.
Actual price = actual cost + fixed fee.
Actual price = $80,000 + $10,000
Actual price = $90,000.
The fixed fee is fixed if the seller is able to complete the work. Be sure to think of the fixed fee as a fixed amount and not a fixed percentage.

46. Your satellite launch project has been going well. The only area that is causing issues is the cost area. The actual cost is already higher than the target cost and the project is not complete. The contract manager tells you that you are nearing the point of total assumption. This concerns both you and your management. The point of total assumption (PTA) is the point when:

a. The actual cost plus the resulting profit is equal to or greater than the price ceiling.
b. The actual cost is equal to or greater than the price ceiling.
c. The resulting profit goes to zero.
d. The seller is taking a loss.

Solution:
Answer (a) is the best answer.
The point of total assumption (PTA) is the point where the actual cost plus the resulting profit is equal to or greater than the price ceiling. If the actual cost alone is equal to or greater than the price ceiling the seller no longer is making a profit. If the actual cost alone is greater than the price ceiling the seller is actually taking a loss.

47. A Cost Plus Incentive Fee (CPIF) Contract has the following parameters:
Target Cost = $100,000
Target Fee = $10,000
Share Ratio 70/30%
Maximum Fee = $12,000
Minimum Fee = $8,000

The seller completes the work for an actual cost of $80,000. What is the final price the seller receives?

a. $84,000
b. $88,000
c. $92,000
d. $96,000

Solution:
Answer (c) is the best answer.
Q. What is the contract type?
Cost Plus Incentive Fee (CPIF).

Q. Do we have an over run or under run and by how much?
The target cost is $100,000.
The actual cost is $800,000.
There is an under run of $20,000.

Q. Will the fee be increased or decreased from the target fee and by how much?
Since there is an under run the seller's fee will increase by the seller's percentage of the under run. The seller's percentage is 30%.
The seller's percentage is always the second number of the share ratio.
The adjustment to the seller's fee will be 30% of $20,000.
Fee adjustment = 30% * $20,000 = $6,000.

Q. What is the actual fee?
Actual fee = target fee + fee adjustment. The $6,000
is being added since there is an under run. The seller
is being rewarded for the overrun.
Actual fee = Target fee + fee adjustment
Actual fee = $10,000 + $6,000
Actual fee = $16,000

Q. Is the actual fee between the minimum fee and the
maximum fee?
No. Therefore, $16,000 cannot be the actual fee. The
actual fee must be between the minimum and the
maximum fee.
The actual fee will be the maximum fee of $12,000.

Q. What is the actual price?
Actual price = actual cost + actual fee
Actual price = $80,000 + $12,000.
Actual price = $92,000.
Since this is a cost plus incentive fee (CPIF) contract
and not a fixed price incentive fee (FPIF) contract there
is no price ceiling to review.

48. Your organization is considering using a Time and materials contract (T&M) for the acquisition of outside experts. You like this contract type as it gives you, the project manager, some flexibility if you need to grow the contract. In general who has more risk under a T&M contract?

a. **The buyer**
b. **The seller**
c. **The risk is shared equally**
d. **Neither party has much risk**

Solution:
Answer (a) is the best answer.
The buyer has more risk on a T&M contract. The primary reason for this is while the rate per hour (or day) is agreed to before the contract is awarded, the exact number of hours (or days) to be billed is not. Therefore, the buyer does know exactly how much he will pay per hour or day, but not the total price of the contract. In some ways this contract type rewards inefficiency. The more hours or days it takes for the seller to complete the work the more the seller will be paid.

49. On many contracts the buyer will audit the seller's accounting records. In fact the buyer is allowed to audit the seller's accounting records on all of the following contract types except?

a. Cost plus fixed fee (CPFF)
b. Cost plus award fee (CPAF)
c. Fixed price incentive fee (FPIF)
d. Firm fixed price (FFP)

Solution:
Answer (d) is the best answer.
On a FFP contract the buyer and seller agree to a fixed price before the seller begins work. The seller is paid that fixed price if he can meet the requirements of the contract. There is no need for the buyer to audit the financial records of the seller because the seller's actual costs are irrelevant to the final price paid. The final price paid is the price agreed to in the contract. Since the seller is reimbursed for actual legitimate costs when using a FPIF, CPAF, or CPFF contract the buyer has the right to audit the accounting records.

50. Your organization sells goods and services to many non-profit organizations around the world. One of your customers is about to award a very large contract. The contract awarded will be a Cost Plus Award Fee (CPAF). You have heard that very large profits, even up to 15%, may be achieved using a CPAF. Which of the following should you be least concerned with before entering into this agreement?

a. The amount of money that could be lost on such a large project.
b. The accounting system required for accurate cost reporting.
c. The award fee is decided unilaterally by the customer.
d. The award fee criteria is often subjective.

Solution:
Answer (a) is the best answer. It is highly unlikely that an organization would lose large amounts of money under a CPAF. With this contract type all legitimate costs are reimbursed and there is an opportunity for a base fee and an award fee. Therefore, we should not be overly concerned with losing money on a CPAF. To use a CPAF we need an accounting system that is auditable. The customer alone decides on how much or how little of the award fee we will receive based on subjective, not objective, criteria.

Bonus Question 1.

You have signed a Cost plus percentage cost (CPPC) contract with a supplier to perform some work for you. The contract parameters include:

Estimated cost: $100,000
Fee Percentage: 10%.

The supplier is able to complete the work for a cost of $80,000. What is the final price paid to the supplier?

a. $80,000
b. $88,000
c. $90,000
d. $110,000

Solution:
Answer (b) is the best answer.

I have this question as a bonus question because I am not sure if there are CPPC questions on the PMP® Exam.

Actual price = actual cost + fee as a percentage of the actual cost.
Actual price = $80,000 + $10% * $80,000
Actual price = $80,000 + $8,000
Actual price = $88,000.

Bonus Question 2.

You have signed a Cost plus percentage cost (CPPC) contract with a supplier to perform some work for you. The contract parameters include:

Estimated cost: $100,000
Fee Percentage: 10%.

The supplier with your permission is able to complete the work for a cost of $120,000. There is no change in scope. What is the final price paid to the supplier?

a. $110,000
b. $120,000
c. $130,000
d. $132,000

Solution:
Answer (d) is the best answer.

I have this question as a bonus question because I am not sure if there are CPPC questions on the PMP® Exam.

Actual price = actual cost + fee as a percentage of the actual cost.
Actual price = $120,000 + $10% * $120,000
Actual price = $120,000 + $12,000
Actual price = $132,000.

Bonus Question 3.
This bonus question comes from:
How to get every Earned Value Management Question right on the
PMP® Exam – PMP Exam Prep Simplified Series of mini-e-books
(50+ PMP® Exam Prep Sample Questions and Solutions
on Earned Value Management)
(AME Group 2014)

You are taking over the role of project manager on a project to build a training facility for horses. Earned value management (EVM) is being used on the project and you have been handed some incomplete information. For your project, the cost performance index (CPI) = 1.2. The actual cost (AC) = $75,000. The planned value (PV) = $60,000. What is the earned value (EV) for this project?

a. $50,000
b. $62,500
c. $72,000
d. $90,000

Solution:
Answer (d) is the best answer.
This is an equation manipulation question. If you look at your equation list you probably do not have an equation to calculate earned value (EV).
In this question we are given the cost performance index (CPI), the actual cost (AC), and the planned value (PV). We are asked to calculate earned value (EV). Do you have an equation with three of these terms including earned value (EV)? Most likely you have the equation:

$CPI = EV/AC$.

We want to solve for EV. Therefore, we want to get EV alone on one side of the equal sign. Multiply both sides of the equation by AC.

AC * CPI = AC * (EV/AC). The two ACs will eliminate each other on the right side of the equation.

AC * CPI = EV.

$75,000 (1.2) = EV

$90,000 = EV

Note that we did not use PV to answer this question. On the exam, we may be given data that we do not need to solve the problem. I call this distractor information.

Bonus Question 4.
This bonus question comes from:

How to get every Network Diagram Question right on the PMP®
Exam – PMP Exam Prep Simplified Series of mini-e-books
(50+ PMP® Exam Prep Sample Questions and Solutions
on Network Diagrams, Crashing, Etc.)
(AME Group Coming late 2014)

**The project schedule shows a duration of 47 weeks.
After careful review management has decided that
the project must finish within 42 weeks. They ask
you and your team to develop a plan to crash the
schedule based on cost. There are five activities on
the critical path that can be crashed. Activity A has
a duration of 8 weeks and can be shortened by 2
weeks for a cost of $4,000. Activity F has a duration
of 9 weeks and can be shortened by 4 weeks for a
cost of $16,000. Activity J has a duration of 12
weeks and can be shortened by 1 week for a cost of
$2,000. Activity K has a duration of 5 weeks and can
be shortened by 2 weeks for a cost of $2,000.
Activity R has a duration of 8 weeks and can be
shortened by 3 weeks for a cost of $9,000.
The activities that should be crashed are:**

a. Activity A and Activity R
b. Activity K and Activity R
c. Activity A and Activity J and Activity K
d. Activity F and Activity J

Solution:

Answer (c) is the best answer. There is a lot of data in
this question. When crashing we want to save the most
amount of time for the least amount of money. For the
PMP Exam I most likely would create a table like the

one below to help me easily solve this problem. Once I have the table I know I need to save five weeks for the least amount of money. Answer (a) will save me 5 weeks for $13,000. Answer (b) will save me 5 weeks for $11,000. Answer (c) will save me 5 weeks for $8,000. Answer (d) will save me 5 weeks for $18,000. Answer (c) is the best answer.

	Current Duration	Weeks to be saved by crashing	Cost of crashing	Cost/week of crashing
Activity A	8 weeks	2 weeks	$4,000	$2,000
Activity F	9 weeks	4 weeks	$16,000	$4,000
Activity J	12 weeks	1 week	$2,000	$2,000
Activity K	5 weeks	2 weeks	$2,000	$1,000
Activity R	8 weeks	3 weeks	$9,000	$3,000

Bonus Question 5.
This bonus question comes from:

How to get every Financial Question right on the PMP® Exam –
PMP Exam Prep Simplified Series of mini-e-books
(50+ PMP® Exam Prep Sample Questions and Solutions
on NPV, IRR, ROI, Etc.)
(AME Group Coming late 2014)

The portfolio review board is conducting a project selection review. They are going to make their decision based on the Net Present Value (NPV) estimates for the projects. The organization has only $100,000 available for investment. Based on the following information which project should they select?
Assume an interest rate of 5%.
Project A - The initial investment = $100,000. The benefit at end of year one = $40,000. The additional benefit at end of year two = $70,000. There are no other benefits.
Project B – The initial investment = $100,000. There is no benefit at the end of year one. The benefit = $42,000 at end of year two. There is an additional benefit = $70,000 at end of year 3.
Which project(s) should they select?

a. **Project A**
b. **Project B**
c. **Both projects since they each have a positive net present value.**
d. **Neither project since they each have a negative net present value.**

Solution
Answer (a) is the best answer.
Project A has a higher NPV than Project B. The NPV of
Project A is a positive number. This means our

estimates show we forecast to make money on this project.

Project A

The Present Value of $40,000 received at the end of year 1:

$PV = FV/(1+i)^t$

$PV = \$40,000/(1.05)^1$

$PV = \$38,095.23$

The Present Value of $70,000 received at the end of year 2:

$PV = FV/(1+i)^t$

$PV = \$70,000/(1.05)^2$

$PV = \$63,492.06$

Therefore the NPV for Project A=

$\$38,095.23 + \$63,492.06 - \$100,000 =$

$+\$1,587.29$

Project B

The Present Value of $42,000 received at the end of year 2:

$PV = FV/(1+i)^t$

$PV = \$42,000/(1.05)^2$

$PV = \$38.095.23$

The Present Value of $70,000 received at the end of year 3:

$PV = FV/(1+i)^t$

$PV = \$70,000/(1.05)^3$

$PV = \$60,468.61$

Therefore the NPV for Project B=

$\$38,095.23 + \$60,468.61 - \$100,000 = -\$1,436.16$

Bonus Question 6.
This bonus question comes from:

How to get every Statistical based Question right on the PMP®
Exam – PMP Exam Prep Simplified Series of mini-e-books
(50+ PMP® Exam Prep Sample Questions and Solutions
on standard deviation, variance, probability, Etc.)
(AME Group Coming late 2014)

You are the project manager for a logging company. This month you are charted to deliver 10,000 units that are 60 centimeters each. Your upper control limit on your process is 63 centimeters. Your lower control limit on your process is 57 centimeters. Approximately what percentage of your units will be above 61 centimeters?

a. 68.3%
b. 31.7%
c. 95.5%
d. 15.9%

Solution
Answer (d) is the beast answer.
15.9 % of the data will be above 61 centimeters.
Here are a few abbreviations we will use.
SD= one standard deviation
UCL = upper control limit
LCL = lower control limit
Also to solve this problem you need the equation for one standard deviation.
$SD = | (UCL-LCL)/6 |$
+/- 1 SD represents 68.23% of the data
+/- 2 SD represents 95.46% of the data
+/- 3 SD represents 99. 73% of the data

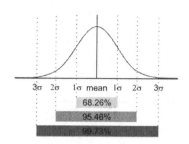

68.26%

95.46%

99.73%

Q- what is one standard deviation?
SD = | (UCL-LCL)/6 |
SD = | (63-57)/6 |= | 6/6 |= 1 centimeter.
Q. What is the mean?
The mean is 60 centimeters.

Q. How many standard deviations is 61 centimeters from the mean?
61 centimeters is +1 standard deviation from the mean.
59 centimeters is -1 standard deviation from the mean.

Q. What percentage of the data falls between 59 and 61 centimeters?
Therefore, 68.3 % of the data will be between 59 and 61 centimeters.

Q. What percentage of the data falls outside of 59 through 61 centimeters?
If 68.3% of the data falls inside of this range than 100% - 68.3% must fall outside of the range.
100% - 68.3% = 31.7%. 31.7% will be outside of 59 centimeters and 61 centimeters.
Q. What percentage of the data falls above 61 centimeters?
Half of 31.7% will be above 61 centimeters and half of 31.7% will be below 59 centimeters.
31.7/2= 15.9% will be above 61 centimeters.
Of course 31.7/2= 15.9% will be below 59 centimeters.

Dear Reader,

I hope you enjoyed my second mini e-book: *How to get every Contract Calculation Question right on the PMP® Exam.* I really enjoy helping people prepare for the PMP® Exam. Most importantly I hope the book is useful to you both for the PMP® Exam and for your project management career.

As you may realize I facilitate workshops on PMP® Exam Preparation. Please see my schedule at www.aileenellis.com and contact me directly at aileen@aileenellis.com if you would like me to come to a town near you.

I would like to request a small favor. If you are so inclined, I'd appreciate a review on Amazon of *How to get every Contract Calculation question right on the PMP® Exam.* Loved it ... Hated it (I hope not) - I would just enjoy hearing your feedback.

As you may have seen with Amazon, reviews can be tough to come by these days. You, the reader, have the power now to make or break a book. If you have time I would love for you to go back to Amazon and write a quick review of the book. Thank you so much for reading my e-book.

To write a review, just go back to the page for my book on Amazon and click on Reviews. Let me know if you would like to see more of these mini e-books. Also, to see all of my books please visit my author page on Amazon.
Regards,

Aileen Ellis, PgMP, PMP